PLANT
DEFENSES

PLANTS THAT POKE

CELESTE BISHOP

New York

Published in 2017 by The Rosen Publishing Group, Inc.
29 East 21st Street, New York, NY 10010

First Edition

Editor: Sarah Machajewski
Book Design: Reann Nye

Photo Credits: Cover Danita Delimont/Gallo Images/Getty Images;
p. 4 grynold/Shutterstock.com; p. 5 Sever180/Shutterstock.com;
p. 6 Videowokart/Shutterstock.com; p. 7 Don Mammoser/Shutterstock.com;
p. 8 GK Hart/Vikki Hart/The Image Bank/Getty Images; p. 9 Michael S. Nolan/
age fotostock/Getty Images; p. 10 Emilio100/Shutterstock.com; p. 11 (thorns)
Anna Chudinovskykh/Shutterstock.com; p. 11 (spines) leungchopan/
Shutterstock.com; p. 11 (prickles) Ganna Biletska/Shutterstock.com;
p. 12 Evgeni_S/Shutterstock.com; p. 13 indigolotos/Shutterstock.com;
p. 14 arka38/Shutterstock.com; p. 15 Christian Vinces/Shutterstock.com;
p. 16 Andriy Markov/Shutterstock.com; p. 17 Stas Moroz/Shutterstock.com;
p. 18 Margaret M Stewart/Shutterstock.com; p. 19 DEA/ARCHIVIO J. LANGE/
De Agostini/Getty Images; p. 20 Manfred Ruckszio/Shutterstock.com;
p. 21 Francois De Heel/Photolibrary/Getty Images; p. 22 yurok/Shutterstock.com.

Cataloging-in-Publication Data

Names: Bishop, Celeste.
Title: Plants that poke / Celeste Bishop.
Description: New York : PowerKids Press, 2017. | Series: Plant defenses | Includes
index.
Identifiers: ISBN 9781499421590 (pbk.) | ISBN 9781499421613 (library bound)
| ISBN 9781499421606 (6 pack)
Subjects: LCSH: Prickles–Juvenile literature. | Plant defenses–Juvenile literature.
Classification: LCC QK650.B57 2017 | DDC 581.4'7–d23

Manufactured in the United States of America

CPSIA Compliance Information: Batch #BS16PK: For Further Information contact Rosen Publishing, New York, New York at 1-800-237-9932

CONTENTS

THAT HURTS!

You're running through a field and all of a sudden—ouch! Something poked your legs, and it hurts! You look down at the ground, and soon it's clear. There's a big, spiky plant in your path. The plant's thorns may have hurt you, but that's their job. They keep the plant safe from animals and people who might hurt it.

Many plants are covered with thorns, spines, or **prickles**. These are meant to **protect** the plant. They'll poke anything that gets too close. Let's explore how and why some plants poke.

The prickles on this thistle plant could really hurt if you touched them.

A SIGN TO STAY AWAY

Thorns, prickles, and spines are common plant defenses. A defense is a way an **organism** protects itself. Thorns and spines are thin and sharp, and they look like something that can hurt you. They tell predators to stay away. Predators who ignore this message find out the hard way that the thorns hurt.

The ability to poke isn't the only plant defense—it's just one of the most **obvious**. Other plant defenses include poison and bad smells. Some plants shrink when they're touched. Others change their colors to blend in with their surroundings. These are all ways plants protect themselves.

AGAVE PLANT

Plants need to protect themselves from predators. This iguana knows not to get too close to this spiky cactus.

FACING CHALLENGES

Plants face many **threats** that challenge their survival. These threats include predators, people, weather, and poor conditions in their **environment**. Defenses protect a plant against these dangers. When a plant is protected, it has a better chance of surviving.

Over time, plants developed adaptations, or changes that helped them face the challenges in their environment. Thorns, prickles, and spines are great adaptations. Long ago, plants that had them may have survived longer than plants without them. These plants were able to survive and pass their adaptation on to the next **generation**.

PLANT POINTER
It takes a long time for an adaptation to become part of a **species**—maybe even thousands of years.

Animals have adaptations, too. Imagine trying to pick up this porcupine. That would hurt!

THORNS, SPINES, PRICKLES

Plants that poke use different kinds of pokers. They can have thorns, spines, or prickles. These **structures** are similar but different.

Thorns are a kind of branch or stem. They're part of a plant's shoot system. A shoot is a young branch that grows off a plant's main stem. They have small leaves that die quickly. The thorns only grow to a certain size and are very hard.

Spines are actually leaves, even if they don't look like them. They're shaped to keep predators away and, commonly, save water. Prickles are sharp growths off a plant's stem.

PLANT POINTER

Prickles are made of the same material as plant stems. It's sometimes called the plant's "skin."

THORNS

SPINES

These structures are all plant parts you're
familiar with. Thorns are branches, spines
are leaves, and prickles are parts of stems.

PRICKLES

PAINFUL ROSE PRICKLES

If roses are known for one thing, it's the painful "thorns" that cover their stems. However, these prickly structures aren't true thorns—people just call them that. Roses actually have prickles.

The prickles on a rose plant are small, sharp structures that can really hurt if you touch them. This defends the plants against herbivores, or animals and bugs that eat only plants. If predators can't get past the prickles, they can't hurt the plant. It works on people, too. Have you ever touched a rose plant? You have to be very careful. Otherwise you'll get poked!

PLANT POINTER
A rose's prickles can be many shapes and sizes.

Roses are known for their beauty, but beware! Their prickles show they can defend themselves.

COOL AS A CACTUS

If there's one plant known for poking, t might be a cactus. These desert plants are covered with sharp spines, which are also called needles. Cactus plants store water nside their stem, which thirsty predators would love to find. However, the sharp spines send a very clear message: "Stay away!" Predators don't want to get a mouthful of needles.

Cactus spines are also a cool adaptation n another way. Plants lose water through their leaves. This is a problem for cacti living n hot, dry places. The plants adapted by replacing bigger leaves with spines. This keeps them from losing too much water.

The spines covering a cactus keep predators away from the store of water inside the stem.

THORNY TRUNK

Do you like to climb trees? It's pretty fun, unless you're climbing a floss-silk tree. Its trunk and branches are covered in sharp thorns. Ouch! This plant developed the hard, wooden growths long ago. They send a clear message: "Keep off!"

The floss-silk tree has beautiful flowers and it also bears, or grows, fruit. The fruit would normally attract animals, such as monkeys, who would like to eat it. However, if animals eat the fruit, the tree can't spread its seeds. Some people think the floss-silk tree developed thorns to keep animals away. This can't be proven, but the thorns are definitely a good defense.

PLANT POINTER
Some scientists **classify** the growths on the floss-silk tree as prickles, not thorns.

No one knows for sure why the floss-silk tree has thorns, but they help protect the trunk's thin bark—especially in young trees.

THISTLE PLANTS

Thistle plants have bright, colorful flowers. Plenty of animals love to eat them. Deer, rabbits, and sheep like to **graze** on thistles that grow in fields. Thistle plants had to develop a defense to keep from being eaten. That's why they have prickles.

Prickles can grow on all parts of the thistle plant, including the stem and leaves. Prickles even grow on the flower itself, especially when the plant is young. That's when they're most likely to be eaten by predators. Be careful if you ever come across a thistle plant. You don't want to be poked by its prickles!

BULL THISTLE

There are many kinds of thistles.
Some look scarier than others!

THAT STINGS!

You might think plants don't grow hair, but the stinging nettle does! It uses its hairs to sting its enemies. Hair isn't the same kind of structure as a thorn, spine, or prickle, but it's still used as a defense.

Tiny hairs cover the stems and leaves of the stinging nettle. The hairs have a sharp tip. Inside, a tube runs from the tip to the body of the plant. When something touches the stinging nettle, the plant releases defensive **chemicals** through its hairs. The chemicals make our skin itch and burn! Some people get red **welts** where the plant touched them.

PLANT POINTER

The stinging nettle can hurt us, but parts of the plant are sometimes used as medicine.

The stinging nettle's hairs are designed to keep wild predators and curious people away.

THE NATURAL WORLD

Plants aren't the only organisms that poke. Plenty of animals and bugs have developed similar adaptations. Porcupines, sea urchins, and the spiny-tailed lizard are animals that many predators don't want to mess with. The crown-of-thorns starfish looks really scary, too! Like plants, their sharp spines protect them from predators that want to eat them.

Plenty of animals sting, too. Bees have a sharp stinger that's used as a **weapon** against enemies. Scorpions sting when they sense danger, and some ants sting, too. Whether it's a spiky animal or thorny plant, poking is an important—and effective—defense.

GLOSSARY

chemical: A substance made inside a plant.

classify: To place in a particular category.

environment: The natural surroundings of a person, plant, or animal.

generation: All the plants of a certain kind that started growing about the same time.

graze: To eat grass in a field.

obvious: Very clear.

organism: An individual plant or animal.

prickle: A sharp growth off a plant's stem.

protect: To keep safe.

species: A group of living organisms that have similar traits.

structure: An arrangement of parts.

threat: Something likely to cause danger.

weapon: Something used to defend oneself or attack something else.

welt: A red mark on the skin.

INDEX

WEBSITES

Due to the changing nature of Internet links, PowerKids Press has developed an online list of websites related to the subject of this book. This site is updated regularly. Please use this link to access the list: www.powerkidslinks.com/plantd/poke